ROBERT EMMET

First published in 2001 by
Mercier Press
5 French Church St Cork
Tel: (021) 275040; Fax: (021) 274969; e.mail: books@mercier.ie
16 Hume Street Dublin 2
Tel: (01) 661 5299; Fax: (01) 661 8583; e.mail: books@marino.ie

Trade enquiries to CMD Distribution 55A Spruce Avenue
Stillorgan Industrial Park Blackrock County Dublin
Tel: (01) 294 2556; Fax: (01) 294 2564
e.mail: cmd@columba.ie

A CIP record for this book is available from the British Library.

ISBN 1 85635 338 9
10 9 8 7 6 5 4 3 2 1

Cover design by Penhouse Design
Printed in Ireland by ColourBooks Baldoyle Dublin 13

ROBERT EMMET

SEAN McMAHON

MERCIER PRESS

CONTENTS

CHRONOLOGY

1778   Born in Molesworth Street, Dublin, youngest son of Dr Emmet, State Physician

1793   Enters Trinity College and distinguishes himself as a sciences student and speaker in the Historical Society; becomes a leader of the United Irishmen in the college and a friend of the poet Tom Moore

1798   Thomas Addis Emmet, his brother, arrested in March; in February, Emmet refuses to attend the 'examination' of John Fitzgibbon, Earl of Clare, the Lord Chancellor, in a personal search for United Irishmen among the students, and has his name removed from the roll of undergraduates

1799   Thomas imprisoned in Fort St George in Scotland; warrant for Emmet's arrest issued but not executed

1800   Has discussions with Thomas in prison about the possibility of another rising and travels on the Continent, visiting Belgium, France, Switzerland and Spain

1801   Act of Union of Great Britain and Ireland becomes law on 1 January

1802   On 25 March, Treaty of Amiens ends Britain's war with France; Emmet has unsatisfactory meetings with Napoleon and Talleyrand and returns to Dublin in October; Emmet's father dies in December

1803   Britain's war with France is resumed on 18 May; Emmet begins to make plans for a rising to coincide with expected French invasion in August;

sets up arms depots using his own money to buy arms; plans badly upset by explosion in Patrick Street depot on 16 July; leads abortive rising on 23 July; is captured on 25 August and executed on 20 September in Thomas Street

1

'MARCHING TO THAT AIR'

There is a legendary story, which may not be entirely apocryphal, that at a provincial performance of a play called *Bold Robert Emmet* in the 1890s there was such dismay when the jury found the hero guilty that there was a riot. The only thing that would placate the angry audience was a different verdict, and on that occasion Robert Emmet, the darling of Erin, walked free. Such an air of theatricality still attaches itself to this most romantic of Irish heroes that it is only with considerable difficulty that a historical perspective on the character can be reached. The sum of his life seems to consist of an evening in July when, dressed in a remarkably theatrical uniform of green, white and gold, he led a murderous rabble through the Liberties of Dublin, of a flight to safety in Wicklow, of a return to keep a tryst with his fiancée and a speech from the dock that has persisted (in an edited and extended form) as one of the great emotional documents of Irish nationalism.

For at least 150 years after his death he was a kind of nationalist saint, free from the taints of age and disillusionment and forever enshrined in the Irish psyche as the young, dashing, handsome, brave hero, lover, orator and martyr. Many Irish boys were christened Emmet in his honour and the coloured print of his handsome profile had almost equal pride of place with the BVM and the Sacred Heart on the walls of Irish kitchens. When Denis Johnston (1900–74) wanted a character for *The Old Lady Says 'No!'* (his 1929 satire on the mores of the Irish Free State), he chose Emmet. Johnston needed someone who would enshrine all that was sentimental and absurdly idealistic in stated Irish aspirations and who would stand in notable contrast to the materialism, hypocrisy and religiosity of the new state. His Speaker, the actor playing Emmet in a play that was a glorious construct of Irish patriotic verse, is injured during the performance and wanders out in costume and character into a Dublin where his epitaph may still not be written. Johnston's original title, *Shadowdance*, was more appropriate to his theme in that the projected Emmet is only connected to the real person by a kind of tacking, as a later Peter Pan had his shadow sewn on by Wendy Darling.

Even in post-historical Ireland, Emmet is still, at least in older people's memory, a meteor – an incandescent falling star. Like Wolfe Tone (1763–98), his more significant predecessor (by fifteen years), he remains a convenient badge of Velcro patriotism which may be attached to all kinds of activist lapels. Yet, as with Tone, his patriotism was of its time: his Ireland freed from British rule would still have needed the patriot (and Protestant) elite to begin to diffuse the pleasanter aspects of Jacobinism, and he was as uneasy with Catholics as were his heroes of Ninety-Eight.

He was born in Dublin in 1778, the youngest son of Robert Emmet, a Cork doctor who had commenced his metropolitan practice in Molesworth Street in 1771 and become physician to the Viceroy. It was there that Emmet was born but the family were able to move to the better address of 110 St Stephen's Green in 1779. Robert was educated in private schools – Oswald's in Dopping Court, near Bride Street, and Whyte's in Grafton Street – and prepared for entrance to Trinity by the Rev Mr Lewis, who kept an exclusive crammer in Camden Street. He entered Trinity on 7 October 1793 when he was fifteen and soon distinguished himself as an orator in the Historical Society, the prestigious college institution that was founded by Edmund Burke and had been the rhetorical proving ground for Tone. In spite of the tradition, he was not especially handsome: he was described as being about five feet six inches in height, with a sallow, pock-marked face, grey, heavy-lidded eyes and a slightly disdainful expression. He was notably quiet and required the stimulus of some political injustice to shake him out of what, to casual observers, seemed inertia.

One of the most famous anecdotes illustrating the remarkable, almost physiological, change that the right spur could effect in him is to be found in the *Memoirs* of his close friend, Tom Moore (1779–1853):

He was an altogether noble fellow, and as full of imagination and tenderness of heart as of manly daring. He used frequently to sit by me at the pianoforte, while I played over the airs from Bunting's Irish collection; and I remember one day when we were thus employed, his starting up as from a reverie while I played the spirited air 'Let Erin Remember the Day' [the lyrics written by Moore himself] and exclaiming passionately, 'Oh that I was at the head of twenty thousand men marching to that air.'

Another aspect of the man is to be found in the pages of one of his earliest biographers, Dr R. R. Madden (1798–1886), who, born in the year of the rising, published *The United Irishmen; Their Lives and Times* in seven volumes between 1842 and 1846. In volume three, a redaction of an earlier life of Emmet issued in 1840, he describes a typical incident in his youth; this incident illustrates the concentration, scientific talent, courtesy and coolness of his subject:

He was in the habit of making chemical experiments in his father's house, and on one occasion nearly fell a victim to his ardour in his favourite pursuit. Mr Patten, the brother-in-law of T. A. Emmet, had been staying at his father's, and on the occasion referred to, had assisted Robert in his experiments. After Mr Patten had retired, the former applied himself to the solution of a very difficult problem in *Friend's Algebra*. A habit which he never relinquished, when deeply engaged in thought – that of biting his nails – was the cause of an accident which proved nearly fatal to him, on the occasion in question. He was seized with the most violent inward pains; these pains were the effects of the poison he had been manipulating, corrosive sublimate, and had, unconsciously, on putting his fingers to his mouth, taken, internally, some portion of the poison. Though fully aware of the cause of his sufferings and of the danger he was in, he abstained from disturbing his father, but proceeded to his library, and took down a volume of an encyclopaedia which was in the room. Having referred to the article 'poison', he found that chalk was recommended as a prophylactic in cases of poisoning from corrosive sublimate. He then called to mind that Mr Patten had been using chalk with a turning lathe in the coach-house; he went out, broke open the coach-house door, and succeeded in finding the chalk, which he made use of, and then set to work again at the puzzling question, which had before baffled his endeavours to solve. In the morning, when he presented himself at the breakfast table, his countenance, to use the language of my informant (who was present) 'looked as small and as yellow as an orange'. He acknowledged to this gentleman that he had suffered all night excruciating tortures, and yet he employed his mind in the solution of that question, which the author of the work acknowledged was one of extraordinary difficulty, and he succeeded in his efforts.

The expertise in science and mathematics, combined with a remarkable rhetorical flair, made him one of the best natural-philosophy men of his time at Trinity. He was personable and popular and included among his friends Richard, the son of John Philpot Curran (1750–1817), the liberal advocate and emancipist who had defended the '98 revolutionaries and had obtained a stay of execution for Tone on the day he cut his windpipe in a suicide attempt.

Although, since the revolutionary upheavals, the Historical Society had considerably less latitude about the topics it might discuss, Emmet was clever (or foolish) enough to apply apparent general topics to the current political situation. In his maiden speech, on the theme of free speech as an essential of good polity, his references to the Greece and Rome of classical times were clearly descriptive of contemporary Dublin. In answer to a conservative rebuttal, he replied with rather too much vigour:

> If a government were vicious enough to put down the freedom of discussion, it would be the duty of the people to

deliberate on the errors of their rulers, to consider well the wrongs they inflicted, and what the right course would be for their subjects to take, and having done so, it then would be their duty to draw practical conclusions.

The speech was made early in 1798 when his brother Thomas was already being shadowed by police spies because of his membership of the United Irishmen. (Tom was arrested by the agents of Viscount Castlereagh (1769–1822), the chief secretary, on 12 March.) At twenty, Robert would not have been a member of the inner councils of the movement, but his enthusiasm for the cause could not be hidden, even if he had wished to conceal it. He had occasion to chide Moore for a piece of dangerous boyish enthusiasm. Though barely a year younger than his hero, Moore seemed almost childish by comparison, and his Catholic grocer father and ambitious mother would have been horrified should their white hope's future be compromised by association with rebels. Still, the Moores were patriotic Irish, and Tom shared the resentment of those who objected to corruption at home and subservience to an uncaring British Parliament.

As he recalled in his *Memoirs*, he 'addressed a letter to "the students of Trinity College" written in a turgid, Johnsonian sort of style, but seasoned with the then-favourite condiment: treason.' His peroration above the signature 'A Patriotic Freshman' read:

> We should all Unite, rally round her [Ireland's] standard and recover our Heaven-born rights, our principles from the grasp of Tyranick masters.

Though meant to please his friend, the letter did not have quite that effect; soon after, while they were out for a walk, he chided Moore 'with an almost feminine gentleness', saying, 'he could not help regretting that the public's attention had been drawn thus to the politics of the University, as it might have the effect of awakening the vigilance of the college authorities and frustrate the progress of the good work . . . which was going on there quietly.'

It was a kindness of Emmet to maintain a personal friendship with a man who, by his own admission, was 'constantly tied to my mother's apron strings' and of little use as a revolutionary. The authorities, indeed, had more than an inkling that the college, as a place where the idealistic young felt they could speak freely, would contain among its undergraduate population some members of the proscribed association. The highly unpopular lord chancellor, John Fitzgibbon, Earl of Clare (1749–1802), and the advocate-general, 'Paddy' Duigenan (who stood out, even in those days, as one who hounded Catholics with the zeal and enthusiasm of a witch-finder), descended upon the college to put the students to the question in February 1798. Moore bumbled his way through the inquisition, retaining some tatters of honour, but Emmet refused to attend and had his name struck off the register.

When the rising did break out, Moore was ill, perhaps judiciously so:

It was while I was confined with this illness that the long and awfully expected explosion of the United Irish conspiracy took place; and I remember well, on the night when the rebels were to have attacked Dublin (May 1798), the feelings of awe produced throughout the city, by the going out of the lamps one after the other, towards midnight.

Whether Emmet was involved is unclear. Dublin played little part in the outbreak and there is no record of his participation in any of the places where fighting took place. It is likely that he was either in hiding in the family home (now at Milltown) or out of the country. He had constructed escape passages, 'priest-holes' and other hiding places into which a person on the run could be stowed or winched up by a system of pulleys and false ceilings. His brother Tom, who was a rather conservative member of the United Irishmen, had been incarcerated on 26 March 1799 in Fort George on the Moray Firth, near Inverness, with seventeen other leaders, including Thomas Russell (1867–1803), Tone's closest friend. (It was originally intended to ship them to America but Rufus King, the American ambassador, had, not unreasonably, objected to the turning of the recently United States into some kind of penal colony.) In spite of the otherwise harsh penology of the time, Tom had contrived to receive visits from his wife, Jane, and family while he was in Newgate and later in Kilmainham; Jane even managed to conceive and bear a child while her husband was a prisoner in Scotland. One of the terms of the 'honourable settlement' was that none of the prisoners should return to Ireland, but there was nothing to prevent Robert from visiting his brother.

2

'DESPARD' REMEDIES

Later romanticisation of Emmet has obscured his dedication to what he considered the necessary means to obtain the freedom that Ireland needed to fulfil her role 'among the nations of the world'. Though the last flicker of the '98 rising had ceased with the death of Tone in November and the execution or imprisonment of its other leaders, there were still disaffected people who could be called to rise again if there seemed to be some hope of success. An actual invasion from France, and not the wishful promise of it, would have pulled the pikes from the rafters and bog-holes where they had been hidden after Wexford and Mayo. Michael Dwyer (1771–1826) was still at large in the Wicklow glens and had let it be known that he would lead his men again should there seem to him to be some chance of success. It is clear that

Emmet discussed another attempt with Tom when he visited him in 1800, having left Ireland because he realised that a warrant had been issued in his name in April of the previous year. The basis of the warrant was the belief that he and others had been reorganising the United Irishmen and had been in touch with the Irish exiles in France. It was also believed that attempts were being made to foment risings in England and Scotland.

Though its adherents were scattered and its rank-and-file followers mainly concerned with such untheoretical matters as the near-famine which had been caused by the lack of corn supplies, there was an active republican movement in Britain. Some middle-class republicans, like their brothers in Belfast and Dublin, had been influenced by the fall of the *ancien régime* in the first, heady days of the revolution in France and they found the court of George III as offensive as that of Versailles. It was true that there was an independent British Parliament with a House of Commons, but it was regarded, with some justice, as oligarchic and corrupt. The main support for republicanism in England, however, was from the working classes, who were forbidden to form any kind of trades union by the draconian Combination Acts of 1799 and 1800. Any attempt at collective bargaining was regarded as subversive, especially in wartime, when the government arrogated to itself all kinds of special powers, including the inter-mittent suspension of habeas corpus. Irish workers in English and Scottish cities were almost *de jure* members and there was strong liaison between the residual United Irishmen in Ireland and the radical United Britons. Most of their activity took the form of food riots, illegal combinations and 'oath-taking' but government intelligence gradually became aware of more concentrated, possibly revolutionary activity.

The name of Colonel Edward Marcus Despard (1751–1803) emerged in agents' reports as that of a possible leader of some kind of armed rising. He was of Irish origin, born in Queen's County, and had served with distinction in both the army and navy. (At his trial, the most famous admiral in Britain, Lord Nelson, spoke in his defence, as a former shipmate of his.) Believing himself cheated and dishonoured by the government while super-intendent in Honduras, he returned to England

and soon joined a revolutionary association known as the London Corresponding Society. He was active in 1797 and 1798 in forming a militant union of English radicals and United Irishmen in the capital. Imprisoned for subversive activity in 1799 and kept in prison in miserable conditions until 1802, he emerged more determined than ever to overthrow the government. His plan was first to seize the king and state officials and then to urge the common people to rise in his support.

Like most of the disaffected of the time, he realised that he required French assistance, the necessary 'partner in revolution' (to use Marianne Elliott's useful phrase) since the war with revolutionary France had broken out in 1793. He had sufficient military experience to understand that no move should be made while the clearly temporary peace held. (The treaty had been signed at Amiens by France, Britain, Holland and Spain on 25 March 1802 but all except the most sanguine realised it marked only a temporary halt to hostilities, which were, in fact, resumed on 18 May 1803.) The authorities were surprised at intelligence reports that he was active so soon after his release. Until recently, it was customary for historians to write him off as a crack-brained adventurer with a grudge, whose scheme was utterly impractical. In fact, the idea of seizing the Tower of London and the Bank of England was of the same pattern as that devised later by Emmet, *mutatis mutandis.* His risky visibility was caused by his concern to hold his ragtag followers in check and wait for a time when his rising could be coordinated with French landings on the English and Irish coasts and another effort by the rejuvenated United Irishmen at home. The autumn of 1803 was agreed as the optimum date for the action. Indeed, at the time of Despard's arrest in November 1802 it had not been finally decided that the Irish venture would be led by Emmet.

There were still many more senior Irish leaders in France, Holland and even England. Tom Emmet, Thomas Russell, Arthur O'Connor (1763–1852) and a dozen others had been released during the peace and made their way eventually to France to join the other Irish exiles. Their relationships that were not characterised by amity caused a deal of scandal to their potential French allies. Emmet found it necessary to use extreme diplomacy in the prevention of a duel between O'Connor and his brother while they were held at Fort George. One of the difficulties of forming a clear picture of Emmet's life at this time is the lack of personal papers for him: he did not keep a journal – his care for personal secrecy ever to the fore – and had little time for letter-writing. It is not clear why, or even when, he emerged as the leader of the rebellion that was called after him. It is likely that, since the grand plan, however imprecise in detail, required a rising in Ireland to coincide with Despard's move in Britain, he was the best candidate: he had the charisma, the mettle, the planning ability and, after his father's death, a small legacy that enabled him to buy shot, powder and timber for the weapons his insurgents would need. He was also free to move about the city without overt inter-ference from the authorities.

The reports of Despard's renewed activity caused the British authorities to begin to build up once more the network of spies and informers which, mainly for reasons of economy, had been allowed to lapse somewhat after the Act of Union in 1800. By the terms of the agreement, the leaders who had been arrested previous to the rising in

1798 were forbidden to return to Ireland, but there was no bar upon their staying in Britain. Further, there was nothing to prevent even known sympathisers from travelling to England in the now-united kingdom. It was the garrulousness of one such Irishman, William Dowdall, who acted as Despard's liaison with Ireland, that may have led to Despard's arrest at the Oakley Arms in Lambeth on 16 November. He was certainly 'imprudent', to use Madden's word, and loud in public conversation, and it was shortly after his last visit to Dublin that Despard was arrested.

The evidence against him and a motley collection of followers, some of them Irish, including two carpenters, a tailor, a shoemaker and two soldiers, was slim, and the jury recommended mercy at the time of their trials in February 1803. Despard denied the charges, especially that of intended regicide, and his execution on 21 February at Newgate was attended by a large crowd of sympathisers. By then, Emmet had been back in Dublin for four months and, among other lessons, had relearned the necessity of guarding against spies and informers. In fact, too great a preoccupation with security was one of the factors that led to the collapse of his own rebellion.

When Emmet went to the Continent from Scotland, however, it was not with any specific intention of becoming the leader of a new insurrection. His travels led him to France, Switzerland, Spain and Holland, in a kind of parody of the Grand Tour that a young gentleman of his class might have made in happier times. He kept no record of his travels but it is clear that he was in touch with Irish exiles in Germany and France. It is almost certain that the details of the next Irish rising were actively discussed. Tom and the other prisoners had been released from Fort George in June 1802, as part of the implicit terms of the Peace of Amiens. It was then that Emmet met Russell, William Henry Hamilton – his niece's husband – and Michael Quigley, the bricklayer from Kildare, who were all to play significant parts in his own rising. Emmet's much-annotated copy of *A History of the Seven Years War* by a Colonel Templehoff is still extant and it is clear that Emmet used his time in Europe to study new ideas about insurgency. These considerations were still at this stage theoretical, as were his designs for exploding beams which could hamper urban cavalry charges and for hinged pikes that could be easily concealed under greatcoats.

The problem of the nature of French involvement in a new rising exercised the expatriate Irish a great deal. It was clear that Napoleon would resume war with Britain at what he considered to be the tactical moment. What the Irish had to consider was the altered nature of French politics. The ideals of the revolution had somehow been mislaid while the First Consul prepared to make himself emperor of most of Europe. In so far as England was enemy to both the radical Irish and France, there was good logistical reason to combine their efforts. Yet there was general distrust among the Irish of Napoleon, whose personal ambitions were not concealed. Emmet understood as well as anyone that no successful rising could be achieved without French assistance, but he was not prepared to exchange British domination for French clientship. It was a matter of pride among the Irish that they would pay their own way, in a sense hiring French arms for the specific task of defeating the garrison forces at home.

Emmet saw Napoleon – the meeting arranged by Talleyrand – not long before he returned to Ireland, and he seems to have impressed the Corsican favourably; the feelings were not reciprocated. Still, the two men had the common objective of injuring England, and Napoleon confided what everyone suspected: that the Peace of Amiens would be short-lived. He ordered the formation of an Irish regiment and gave not-very-precise assurances that there would eventually be a French invasion. Though there is no documentary evidence for this, it seems clear that by then the plan for simultaneous risings in England and Ireland to coincide with French landings had been agreed, at least in broad terms. This would explain Despard's risky public reappearance and give a rational basis to Emmet's hope that, with the symbols of British authority in rebel hands, the ordinary people of both countries would rise 'against tyranny'. They might even produce a similar effect to the fall of the Bastille fourteen years earlier.

When Emmet returned home to Dublin, sometime in the autumn of 1802, it was as much for personal reasons as with any intention of leading another rising. He moved freely about the city and gave no impression that he was engaged in any conspiracy. He was still a member of the United Irishmen and had probably indicated that he would serve, in whatever capacity, should the time come for revolt. He had renewed his old friendship with Richard Curran and was invited to the Priory – the house that Richard's father had built in Rathfarnham – as a matter of course. (Curran took pride in being the 'Prior' of the 'Monks of the Screw', the convivial society he had founded with Grattan and Charlemont, and continued the metaphor in naming his house.) Though never a member of the United Irishmen, he was a noted liberal and would have known of Emmet's connection with the movement. It was soon obvious to the father, whose jovial mien away from home was dramatically different from the dark persona he presented to his family, that young Emmet's frequent visits had more to do with his second daughter, Sarah, than with his analyses of Ireland's wrongs.

3

A SATURDAY EVENING IN JULY

Dr Emmet died early in December 1802 and left
his youngest son a legacy of £3,000. By then, he
was lodging at the house of Mrs Palmer in
Harold's Cross, having just missed arrest in
Milltown by Swan, Town-Major Sirr's deputy. Sirr
(1746–1841) had become the effective head of the
policing of the city in 1796, filling a post earlier
held by his father. It was he who had apprehended
Lord Edward Fitzgerald, one of the key figures in
the intended rising on 19 May 1798, and was to
prove Emmet's nemesis also. Hamilton was at this
stage the senior active member of the conspiracy
and introduced Emmet to Myles Byrne (1780–
1862), who had fought in Wexford in '98 and
could command an effective band of Wexford
men, some of whom had settled in south Dublin.
Emmet was already in touch with Michael Dwyer,

and maintained contact by means of Dwyer's nephew, Arthur Devlin, who was the brother of his housekeeper, Anne (1780–1851). Michael Quigley (who was intended as the mobiliser for Kildare) and Russell were still in France, but Jemmy Hope (1764–c. 1846), the Templepatrick weaver who had fought with McCracken in Antrim, was working in the Liberties and anxious to resume the old struggle.

Though it is not clear exactly when Emmet found himself leader of the proposed insurrection, he undoubtedly contributed to the details of the final plan and was brimming over with ideas for new armaments and tactics. Just as Despard intended to take over the Tower of London, the Bank and the Treasury building, and wait for a populist rising, Emmet intended first to secure the Castle, as the actual and symbolic centre of British rule. Strategically placed buildings, notably the Pigeon House explosives store, the Royal Barracks at the south end of the Phoenix Park, the artillery barracks at Islandbridge, the old Customs House at the North Wall and the army command post at Mary Street, would also be seized to prevent any attempt to retake the Castle. The streets to the west of the Castle would be barricaded with chains and carts. The milder equivalent of Despard's supposed intention to kill George III was to be the seizure and imprisonment of the Lord Lieutenant by the Dublin insurgents.

The manpower for the initial strike would consist of Emmet's own, mainly working-class, recruits, partly organised by Hope; Quigley's men from Kildare, who would arrive from the west and join the colony of Kildare men already settled in Dublin; and Byrne's Wexford troop, who would assemble at Coal Quay. Dwyer, who had been out in '98 and had evaded capture in the Wicklow glens, had made it clear that he would lead his men only after it was clear that the Castle had been taken; even then, he was anxious that some proof of French involvement should be shown. The next stage should consist of spontaneous risings in the provinces, once the provisional government had been established.

Not long after his return home, Emmet was invited to dinner in the Mount Argus mansion of John Keogh, one of Dublin's richest Catholics, at which Curran was a guest. In the conversation after the meal, the host wondered what support

Emmet believed there would be for a general rising. He asked him how many counties would rise, and received the answer, 'Nineteen.' It is impossible to evaluate such optimism. More realistic and encouraging was Curran's response that two counties, if reliable, would be a sufficient reason to risk the venture. In fact, Emmet depended upon the perhaps enthusiastic enthusiasm of the committed, believing Quigley when he said that Kildare would surely rise. Byrne and Dwyer were more experienced and less sanguine. They knew precisely how many men would follow them and they reserved the right to deploy these forces as it seemed best to them. Russell and Hope believed that the old spirit of United Irishmen was still high in the North, but they had been out of touch for too long. The fate of McCracken and Munro had permanently sobered up the majority of Ulstermen.

The phrase 'delirium of the brave' was used by Yeats in his poem 'Easter 1916' to describe the attitudes of the insurgents; the same might equally be applied to Emmet. Apart from generous contributions by Phil Long, a merchant who lived in Crow Street near the Theatre Royal, the adventure was entirely financed by him, using the

£3,000 left him by his father. The support promised by other substantial citizens did not materialise but by March 1803 there was no possibility of his turning back. A number of properties close to the Castle – in Dirty Lane off Thomas Street, Patrick Street, Winetavern Street and Smithfield north of the river – were acquired as depots. The timber for pikes, which could be quite effective weapons for street-fighting at a time when reloading muskets was a slow and tedious business, was conveyed openly by Myles Byrne from his brother-in-law's timber yard, and he was also able to hire a good gunsmith. Some of the timber was sawn into beams and hollowed out to make the exploding logs that Emmet set such store by. He also experimented successfully with rockets that would have had devastating effects in the narrow streets and lanes around the Castle. (These were identical to those devised by Sir William Congreve (1772–1828) in 1808 and used by the British to good effect against Napoleon and in the war with America in 1812.)

It was this preoccupation with explosives that led to the first of a series of disasters that was to turn a practical plan into a farcical rout. (Russell afterwards said that the only surprising thing about the rising was its lack of success.) On 16 July Johnstone, Emmet's assistant bomb-maker, caused an accidental explosion in the Patrick Street depot. The conspirators believed that it was only a matter of time before the authorities would uncover the extent of the plotting. In fact, the police search was cursory and no immediate action was taken. It was only in the fierce recriminations between the army, police and government officials, and between Dublin and London, that took place after the trial of Emmet that the ineptitude of the authorities was revealed. It was decided by Emmet, Byrne and Russell that the rising should begin one week later and that the time in between should be spent in accelerated preparations.

Russell had arrived back from Paris in April and, with a rather sentimental memory of old times with Tone in Belfast, remained convinced that the stalwart United Irishmen should rise again in the place where the society had been founded. He, Hamilton and Hope (whose task it was to have been to rouse the Coombe weavers) were sent north to announce the bringing forward of the date. Quigley could vouch for his Kildare men, and Byrne's veterans had already been summoned to their agreed rendezvous in Coal Quay. Since everyone agreed that many of the plans of the '98 rising had been betrayed by government spies and informers, the need for concealment was understood to be paramount. It worked only too well: no one was quite sure exactly what was to happen and there were no contingency plans or fall-back positions. What was to prove most disastrous of all was the lack of a workable communications system. For example, the messenger sent to rouse Michael Dwyer stopped in an inn on the way and did not meet his quarry until Sunday 27 July, by which time the flash-in-the-pan rising was over.

The Kildare men began arriving into the city late on Friday evening, to join their fellow countymen who resided west of the Castle. This vanguard party was not impressed by Emmet or his new-fangled weapons; they decided that there were not enough firearms – he had, at most, eighteen blunderbusses and four muskets. Emmet, in desperation, agreed to try to buy more, sending to Crow Street to his friend Phil Long for £500. The messenger was unable to find him, and

Emmet gave what little he had left to buy a few pieces. By then, many of the Kildare men had made their way out of the city again, turning back any of the later arrivals from Kildare that they met on the Naas road. They had been told that the rising had been postponed till the following Wednesday. (Those leaders who had talked to Emmet in Thomas Street the previous evening and listened as he agonised about whether they should wait, after all, for a French landing were understandably confused and could not reasonably order their men to stay.) Those who did stay hung around the alehouses, making it clear to all that something was going to happen that evening. Already, one of the Castle spies, Edward Clarke, who lived at Palmerston outside the city, had reported that some of his employees had told him that they were going to Dublin to take part in a rising and needed their pay.

By now the Castle authorities should have been on the alert. Earlier in the day, Nason Browne, an innkeeper at Islandbridge, had told the guard that he had overheard four men at breakfast discussing the plan of attack. One was the same Dowdall whose indiscreet and easily audible conversation had accelerated the arrest of Despard. It is clear that the authorities had lowered their guard in the relatively peaceful time after the Act of Union was passed: the highly organised secret-service system of spies and informers that had been so successful in the previous decade had been allowed to fall inactive. Notably successful spooks like Leonard McNally (1752–1820) still kept up their contacts, and Town-Major Sirr never relaxed his watchfulness, but in many cases the government figures refused to be shaken out of their disregard. They were determined to play down the importance of the rumours; the Castle gates were still open at 7.30 on the Saturday evening.

The sequence of incompetence and bad luck continued. Copies of the proclamation of the provisional government, which Emmet and Long had composed, arrived from the printers, but the ladders needed to scale the rear walls of the Castle did not. The detonators for the explosive beams were forgotten and it was not possible to tell which slow matches were primed and which were not. The main Dublin command intended to travel from the depot in Thomas Street to the Castle in six coaches that they believed would carry them safely past the gates. As the six empty coaches clattered through the streets, the outrider Ned Conlon was challenged by a mounted army officer who wondered what their purpose was. Conlon drew his pistol and shot him. Thereupon the coachmen, who were not part of the plot, turned and drove their vehicles rapidly from the place. Next, Michael Quigley appeared, screaming that the soldiers were out and making their way to the depot. In fact, the streets were clear, and Emmet, who had been on the point of aborting the business, afterwards wondered about Quigley's motive in spreading the false story. Deciding to die in battle rather than remain to be taken captive, Emmet donned his gorgeous uniform of plumed hat, white breeches and green coat with gold epaulettes and, with a few companions, sallied forth into Thomas Street.

It was a Saturday night in a city that was unusually crowded. There was an abundant supply of pikes lying outside the depots and it was not long until a drunken and armed mob was loose. Emmet and his men could not hope to control them but he could make sure that Myles Byrne's

Wexford men were not put in pointless danger. The rocket that was to have been their signal as they waited in Coal Quay was not fired. Emmet and his party headed for their headquarters in Butterfield Lane in Rathfarnham, leaving the streets round the Castle full of rioters. It was quite fortuitous that they stopped and surrounded the coach of Arthur Wolfe, Lord Kilwarden, the lord chief justice – and a man unusually noted for his humanity – who was on his way to an emergency meeting in the Castle. He and his nephew, the Rev Richard Wolfe, were piked to death; his daughter, who cowered terrified inside the coach, was spared and escorted safely to the Castle. In all, the evening saw fifty deaths.

Outside of Dublin, there was no activity at all. On Sunday the twenty-fourth, Russell, in spite of failing to find the promised 'stout guard of County Down men' in Newry, issued a pamphlet to 'the men of Erin' as 'general-in-chief of the Northern district' assuring them that 'in Dublin, in the West, in the North and in the South the blow has been struck at the same moment'. He had later tried in vain to raise a force in Loughinisland, near Downpatrick, and, though Hope and Hamilton found a few stalwarts ready to fight in places like Kells, Broughshane and Templepatrick in County Antrim, there were not enough of them to constitute a fighting force. Stephen Wall, Russell's man in Belfast, stated baldly: 'The town will not rise.' Limerick, Cork and the West, though full of rumours about possible action, were equally quiet.

On the following Friday the government suspended habeas corpus, the legislation being rushed through in a single day. Dublin remained under martial law and on 21 August a curfew and an order requiring householders to post the names of occupants on front doors were imposed by the lord mayor. At last the authorities were geared to bringing the insurrectionists to justice. Sirr, who had done his best to alert William Marsden, the under-secretary (who had responsibility for security), and had tried to communicate his suspicions to Philip Hardwicke, the lord lieutenant, was given the task of arresting the culprits. As ever with officialdom, they made him feel that he was in some way responsible for the trouble in his city but his stoical reaction was to make every effort to apprehend this latest disturber of His Majesty's peace.

4

HAROLD'S CROSS

One of the elements that give an operatic air to Emmet's career is his love affair with John Philpot Curran's second daughter. In a life in which many details are quite obscure, there seems no doubt that she was the reason he remained in Ireland when he could easily have escaped to France. Emmet had fallen instantly in love with her on his return to Ireland in the autumn of 1802, and the father's disapproval, mediated through her older sister Amelia, had the usual effect of increasing the determination of the lovers to laugh at metaphorical locksmiths. Sarah was perhaps six years younger than Emmet and, though light-hearted, even schoolgirlish in his company and in her letters to him, had a history of 'breakdowns' which began when she was thirteen. Her mother, weary of neglect and a temperamental husband, had eloped with a clergyman called Sandys and her favourite daughter had taken the desertion very hard. She was slow to return Emmet's passion, offering him instead an unspecific 'friendship'.

The house in Butterfield Lane that Emmet rented in April as Mr Ellis made it easier for them to meet, and his servant Anne Devlin acted as postman for what was a regular correspondence. They also managed to keep in touch while he was in hiding in Harold's Cross. Sarah and he must have discussed his plans and, though she naturally regarded the venture with concern, there was also an element of excitement and larkiness about the prospect of it. It is clear too that by the time of the rising any reluctance on her part about expressing her stronger feelings had gone. In one of her letters (undated but probably written after the debacle) which was found on Emmet's person, she writes with a lover's intimacy: 'And such is the perfect confidence that I feel subsists between us that I have no fear of misconstruction on your part of any uneasiness I feel.' She goes on to express her concern to find 'from you how matters stand at present'. The letter has an air of caution, with two admonitions to Emmet 'to burn it instantly' and contains the tantalising intelligence that 'I passed the house you are in twice this day, but did not see you. If I thought you were in safety, I would be comparatively happy, at least. I cannot help listening to every idle report'.

The letter was written over a period of sixteen hours ('I believe you will find out that I began and ended this letter in very different moods. I began it in the morning and it is now near two at night.' Its penultimate sentence seems to be in code: 'I long to know how your wife and *ten small* children are.' Enigmatic references in love letters are notoriously hard to decipher and historians and biographers have failed to agree on the significance of Sarah's concluding sentence. It may refer to Anne Devlin who was arrested and tortured soon after Emmet fled, and to other friends, including Quigley and Nicholas Stafford, the baker from James Street who had supplied quite a few recruits. These had gone with Emmet first to Butterfield Lane and thence deeper into the Wicklow hills and glens.

During the week after the rising they rested in inns of varying degrees of safety, missing arrest by a hair's breadth. On the Friday they agreed to separate and it was than that Emmet decided to stay in Ireland, needing to see Sarah and anxious to prevent her from being made anxious or put in danger from Sirr's men. He was sheltered by Mrs Palmer and spent the remaining weeks of his freedom in her house, calling himself Hewitt. It was a pleasant villa on the edge of the city with a walled garden in which he took his exercise in the warm August days. His visitors included Phil Long and his old friend John Patten, the brother of Tom's wife, who urged him to make his escape to France. Myles Byrne implied that it was his duty personally to urge the French government to do something for Ireland. Emmet was rather shy about meeting Byrne; he wondered if the Wexford man might blame him for leaving him and his men in possible danger while he fled to the safety of the mountains. Byrne not only accepted his explanation for the confusion and the rocket signal that never came but commended Emmet's plan. Though vitiated by ill-luck, false

alarm and poor communication, 'Not for cen-
turies had Ireland so favourable an opportunity
of getting rid of the cruel English yoke,' as
Byrne later wrote.

Emmet, persuaded by Byrne's enthusiasm
and generosity, agreed to try to escape but he
had left it too late. Sirr had let it be known that
the reward for information would be very
generous; he was soon able to narrow the field
and had reason to suppose that his quarry was
to be found somewhere between the city and
Rathfarnham. He almost certainly knew about
the attachment to Sarah Curran and, suspecting
that Anne Devlin was their courier, had her
arrested again. This time he tried to bribe her,
offering her £500 – a large sum of money, which
would have made her remaining forty-eight
years rather more comfortable than they in fact
turned out to be. When she refused to give
information, she was held in solitary confinement
in Kilmainham for a year and might have died
– as did her father and brother – but for the
kindness of the wife of one of the turnkeys, who
risked occasionally removing her from her cell
and taking her to her own apartments. The wine

and proper food provided there restored her to some semblance of normality. She was finally released in 1805, having suffered as much from the attrition of Dr Trevor, the superintendent of the jail, as from Sirr's minions, who had prodded her with bayonets and half hanged her. Madden sought her out in 1843 when she was sixty-three and had been living in poverty. Together they visited the house in Butterfield Lane where Emmet had lived and in the yard of which she had been tortured.

Sirr arrived at the Palmer house on 25 August and, after a short struggle, Emmet was arrested. He was anxious from the start that none of the Palmers should suffer on his account and was particularly concerned to keep Sarah from being involved. The Castle authorities were relieved that the man who, as he wrote in a letter to his brother, had given a scuffle 'the respectability of an insurrection' was in their hands. Their main purpose was self-exculpation: they had been caught off guard and could have been faced with a serious breach of civil order if not an actual respectable insurrection. Emmet's venture had been defeated by ill-luck and inexperience rather than by an alert counter-revolutionary force. Lord Lieutenant Hardwicke, Chief Secretary William Wickham and Marsden were determined to blur the fact that they had ignored police intelligence and the reports of such long-established informers as McNally. In this matter Marsden was especially culpable. Fox, the commander-in-chief of the army, had not been told of the explosion in Patrick Street that had forced Emmet to bring forward the date of his rising. It is one of the fascinating 'ifs' of history to consider what might have been the result of such meticulous and imaginative planning if he had been able to wait until a more appropriate time.

In this respect, the town authorities were blameless, and Sirr's insistent reports were ignored partly because of his anomalous position as the head of the civic police force and also because of aristocratic condescension towards a relentless junior officer. The army was remarkably slow to respond, taking action only on the day of the outbreak. (It was his anxiety to attend the emergency meeting called by Hardwicke that led Kilwarden into the path of his killers.) It was, however, the Castle oligarchy who were correctly blamed for incompetence and worse. Emmet's arrest had given them the opportunity for a face-saving piece of counter-propaganda, and his arraignment was going to be what later ages would call a show trial. Apart from stating his name, the accused said virtually nothing. He would give no names of colleagues, nor comment about any French involvement in the rising. The one lever the interrogators had was the letters from Sarah that Sirr had found on him when he was arrested; in spite of her sound advice to destroy them, he carried them with him everywhere. The interrogaters wanted to know the name of the writer and warned that, unless he supplied information about arms dumps or, as did his brother and others of the '98 leaders, gave details without names, his correspondent might be arrested for high treason.

It was the one prospect that visibly agitated the prisoner and made him susceptible to entrapment by the government when he was returned to Kilmainham. An apparently kindly warder called George Dunn offered to take a letter to his cousin St John Mason, who might thereby effect the means of his escape. The letter was delivered, and a plan, involving an immediate payment of £500 to Dunn for his connivance and a further £500 after a successful escape, was devised. The details of the scheme were communicated to Wickham by Trevor, and Mason was arrested. The sorely tried Emmet, disappointed by the failure of the plan and deeply concerned about Sarah, responded eagerly to Dunn's offer to deliver any other message he might like to write. This last letter expressed his worries about her: 'I was sure you were arrested, and could not stand the idea of seeing you in that situation . . . Do not be alarmed; they may try to frighten you, but they cannot do more.' He addressed it to 'Miss Sarah Curran, the Priory, Rathfarnham' and within the hour it was in the hands of a very surprised Wickham.

Emmet had hoped that Sarah's father would defend him as he had the '98 leaders but, on hearing of Sarah's involvement, he refused and, in a characteristic dark rage, turned on his daughter. When Sirr arrived out at the Priory early on the morning of 11 September, Curran was not at home and Sarah was still in bed. She hurried downstairs, to be informed by Sirr that she was under arrest as an accomplice of Emmet. She collapsed in a kind of fit and, in the resulting confusion Amelia, the older sister, took the opportunity of taking Emmet's letters from Sarah's secret cache and burning them. The resourceful Sirr was able to save a few evidential scraps with Emmet's handwriting on them. When Curran returned home and learned what had happened, his anger was intense. He cursed Sarah but she was too *distraite* to notice. He had never shown much love for her, dispatching her to Lismore to stay with the local rector when his wife ran away and hoping that she would soon recover from the embarrassment of her breakdown. His own emotional domestic life had ended with the tragic death of his favourite daughter, Gertrude, who had fallen from a window. He had been heartbroken, insisting that she be buried in the orchard, where her grave would be visible from his study.

Another cause of his spleen was the fear that any association, however tenuous, with Emmet would damage his own career. Though liberal and effective in his defence of rebels, and an eloquent enemy of the Act of Union, he had ambitions to be made a judge – and the authorities had been making the right kinds of noises. (Kilwarden, Curran's friend and fellow 'monk', had been the go-between.) Refusal to defend Emmet was inevitable and Wickham was then able to assure him that no action would be taken against his errant daughter. She was effectively forbidden the house and, shortly after the death of her lover, went to live with friends in Glanmire, near Cork. Cooper Penrose was a Quaker, a member of a family which, as the name suggests, originally came from Cornwall. He and his wife, Elizabeth, sheltered Sarah in their home, Wood Hill, for the next two years; it was there that she met Captain Sturgeon, whom she eventually married.

Emmet was greatly relieved when he heard that Sarah would not be arrested but he was sorely disappointed that he would not be defended by the best counsel of the time. He was pleased when Leonard McNally and Peter Burrowes were appointed. McNally had been a United Irishman and was an entertaining companion, having been in his time a grocer,

playwright and successful songwriter, still re-
membered as the author of 'Sweet Lass of
Richmond Hill'. It was only after his death that
he was revealed as one of the most successful
government agents. Burrowes too was a Castle
informer and it is clear that the prosecution
were apprised of the defence case in advance. It
mattered very little; with Sarah at least physically
safe, Emmet was interested only in his vindi-
cation as a patriot and in the opportunity to ask
for the charity of the world's silence.

5

GREEN STREET AND THOMAS STREET

Emmet's trial began and ended in Green Street courthouse on Monday 19 September 1803, almost two months after the night of the rising. The presiding judge was the notorious John Toler, Baron Norbury (1745–1831), once solicitor-general and later ennobled for his active and cynical support of the pro-Union faction. Notably anti-Catholic, he represented all that was objectionable about the venal Dublin establishment. A coarse bully, weak in jurisprudence and with a justified reputation as a hanging judge, he was later the main target of Daniel O'Connell, whose relentless pursuit of him caused the judge to resign. Once, when Norbury and Curran were riding past the Newgate gallows, Norbury asked him where he would be if that scaffold were to have its due.

Curran replied, 'Riding alone, my lord!' The choice was deliberate, since the authorities required not only exoneration for themselves but humiliation for their prisoner.

In his opening address, Standish O'Grady, the attorney-general, did his best to diminish the prisoner, anxious to belittle him in the eyes of the populace, with whom he had already assumed something of the standing of a martyr. He failed to detract from Emmet's innate nobility; this fact was further emphasised when the witnesses for the prosecution were, on Emmet's instruction, not challenged by his lawyers. This was helpful to at least one of them, Joseph Palmer, the son of his landlady at Harold's Cross, who visibly showed his reluctance as he confirmed that Emmet had stayed there. The last of the prosecution witnesses was Sirr, who described his capture and arrest. The court was surprised when McNally announced that he would make no case. It was even more surprised when, against all normal procedure, one of O'Grady's colleagues, William Conyngham Plunkett, an old family friend of the Emmets, launched a diatribe against the man who would even think of separating Ireland from Great Britain:

'God and nature have made the two countries essential to each other; let them cling to each other to the end of time.' Emmet was incensed at the length of the superfluous speech but bore a final personal attack without apparent concern. Plunkett became solicitor-general two months later.

The jury returned a verdict of 'guilty' without leaving the box, and McNally, ever the sensitive friend, requested that, in view of the hour, sentence might be put off till the next day. This was refused, and a clearly fatigued Emmet was asked the usual question as to whether he had anything to say why judgement of death should not be passed upon him. The peroration to the speech that followed has become part of the nationalist tradition and it confirms everything Moore says about Emmet's rhetorical skills. Its eloquence, sincerity and euphony moved even Norbury; yet the main text is in ways far more interesting. The charge of being an emissary of France he dismissed:

> It is false. I did not wish to join this country to France. I did join – I did not create – the rebellion; not for France, but for

liberty . . . If the French come as a foreign
enemy, oh, my countrymen, meet them on
the shore with a torch in one hand and a
sword in the other. Receive them with all
the destruction of war – immolate them in
the boats before our native soil shall be
polluted by a foreign foe.

It was sensational stuff and everyone, judges and
all, listened intently; but when he went on to say
that the object was to effect a separation from
England, Norbury interrupted. Each time Emmet made to criticise England, Norbury inter-
vened, calling his explanations treason, to which
the court was not required to listen. Interruptions
in steadily increasing anger continued until the
prisoner reached the set-piece that begins with:
'My lord, you are impatient for the sacrifice . . . '
It finished with the great *glissando:*

When I am prevented from vindicating
myself, let no man dare calumniate me.
Let my character and my motives repose
in obscurity and peace till other times
and other men can do them justice; *Then*

shall my character be vindicated. *Then* may my epitaph be written. I have done.

When he sat down, a visibly moved Norbury pronounced the sentence of hanging and beheading to take place the next day. As Madden notes with strong emphasis: 'When the prisoner was removed from the dock it was about ten o'clock at night!!!' Just before he left the dock, McNally leant forward and kissed him on the cheek. Emmet was taken back to Newgate but at midnight he was moved in heavy chains to Kilmainham, because of its greater security. The government had heard a rumour that there was a plan to free him. Here the governor, John Dunn, took off the chains which had caused his wrists to bleed and, seeing how exhausted he was, gave him food and drink, and a cell with a fire and a decent bed. Emmet slept well and spent the time left to him next morning in writing letters: to Richard Curran, asking forgiveness ('I have deeply injured you, I have injured the happiness of a sister that you love . . . I have no excuse to offer, but that I meant the reverse'); to Wickham a kind of exoneration of the administration that he probably agreed to write; to Tom, giving a detailed account of the rising and a shorter, more personal note addressed to him and his wife, Jane, which included 'one dying request' that, should Sarah prove to have no one else to care for her, they should 'treat her as my wife and love her as a sister'.

The egregious McNally, his only permitted visitor, broke the news to him of his mother's death (on the day of his arrest) in typically dramatic fashion. He asked Emmet if he should like to see his mother and said, turning his thumb to the ceiling, 'You shall see her tonight.' Emmet gasped, 'It is better so', and bowed his head. McNally later reported to the authorities that Emmet had told him of a detailed plan recommended to Napoleon by the Irishmen in France involving a French landing in Galway Bay and the securing of Derry city and County Donegal, thus offering a threat to Scotland where there was hope of support against the English. He believed that, if his trial had been put off for even ten days, such a landing might have saved him. It is said that, after McNally left, Emmet occupied himself with drawing a picture of a body with a severed head.

About half past one in the afternoon, Emmet was taken by carriage to Thomas Street, where a scaffold had been erected outside the then-forty-year-old St Catherine's Church. His route had been a little circuitous, crossing the river at Islandbridge and back again at the Queen's Bridge. The journey took nearly an hour and a half, through a crowded and silent city. On the platform he was granted the right to indicate by the dropping of his handkerchief when he was ready. Blindfolded and with the rope round his neck, he seemed to delay as if he somehow expected rescue. Twice asked by the hangman if he were ready, he replied that he was not, but a third refusal was cut off. After a while the executioner, declaring him dead, cut off his head with a butcher's knife and, holding it by the hair, declared to the crowd: 'This is the head of Robert Emmet, a traitor.' The body was put in a plain deal coffin and taken to Kilmainham, where it lay for relatives to claim it. The members of his immediate family were dead or in exile and none of his friends was bold enough to approach.

A plaster death mask was made by James Petrie but it is not clear what happened to the head afterwards, nor is it known where the body was finally buried. It was first interred in a shallow grave in Bully's Acre, a kind of Potter's Field for criminals and paupers near Kilmainham, but it was exhumed from there and reburied, perhaps in St Michan's in Church Street, in the vaults of which Henry and John Sheares, United Irishmen who had been hanged in July 1798, also lay. It was there that the Emmet family had worshipped. Other suggestions have been St Anne's in Dawson Street, St Peter's in Aungier Street and St Paul's in North King Street. The cherished detail of dogs licking up the blood that seeped through the planks and of women dipping their handkerchiefs in it must have been true of other executions that had taken place there in previous weeks but already Emmet's story was moving out of history into legend, if not actual hagiology.

The best example of this evolution may be seen in the fact that the most quoted sentence from the piece of rhetoric known since as 'Robert Emmet's Speech from the Dock' was not in fact spoken by him. The peroration, 'When my country takes her place among the nations of the earth, then and not till then, let my epitaph be written', seems to have been added in other times by other men. It makes a better rhetorical flourish and it is truly his in everything but fact.

5

'O BREATHE NOT HIS NAME'

Tommy Moore published the first edition of his *Irish Melodies* in April 1808. It included a ballad called 'O Breathe Not His Name', which, to those who knew, was a clear tribute to his dead friend. Emmet was also the inspiration for the more famous 'The Minstrel Boy to the War Has Gone' and for 'Lay His Sword by His Side', which ends with the appropriate apostrophe:

> Then at Liberty's summons, like lightning
> let loose,
> Leap forth from thy dark sheath again!

In the circumstances, these were quite daring things for the apron-stringed mother's boy to write, but he became much more courageous as he grew older – and much more outspoken in his nationalism, to the extent of finding Daniel O'Connell too complaisant. Emmet stayed ever fresh in his memory: there are twenty references to him in Moore's *Memoirs, Journals and Correspondence* (1853–6). Typical is the entry for 24 September 1838 (thirty-five years after the patriot's death), which describes his being at dinner in the Castle (at which a fellow guest was Sir Arthur Wellesley, the son of the Duke of Wellington, 'who listened attentively') and concludes with the words: 'Well, thank God, I have lived to pronounce a eulogium upon Robert Emmett [sic] at the Irish Chief Secretary's [Sir Henry Hardinge's] table.'

The fate of Emmet continued to trouble the consciences of some of the more liberal Whigs who remained Moore's patrons. Emmet's innate gentility, idealism and dignity during his trial and on the scaffold, together with the thrilling nature of his speech in court and his relative youth, all helped raise him out of the ruck of terrorism. (I say 'relative' youth because Napoleon was only nine years older than him and maturity came earlier in times of shorter life expectancy.) Moore's threnody for Sarah, 'She is far from the land where her young hero sleeps' (written for the 1811 edition), however, was for its highly appreciative English audience not only intensely moving but unspecific enough not to cause the politically unaware unease.

The opening lines of the tributary ballad are a direct response to Emmet's own request about memorials:

> O breathe not his name, let it sleep in the
> shade,
> Where cold and unhonoured his relics
> are laid;

Even more significant and prophetic was the closing couplet:

> And the tear that we shed, though in
> secret it rolls,
> Shall long keep his memory green in our
> souls.

In just five years – far less time than for more significant colleagues – Emmet had become a romantic icon.

The strongest element of this reputation lay in the story of the blighted love affair. Sentimental and largely untrue details attached themselves to the legend: Emmet had managed to see Sarah in prison; she had watched from a curtained coach the savagery of the execution; she managed to slip out of the Priory to visit the grave. In the patriotic melodrama which begins Denis Johnston's play, the character is arrested not at his lodgings in Harold's Cross, where the real Emmet was found, but after a balcony scene that owes a lot to Shakespeare, at his lover's home in Rathfarnham. The truth is that, until some kind of recovery of health began with the Penroses, Sarah was in no fit state to manage any kind of independent initiative. She recovered in time and was married in the local church in Glanmire on 24 November 1805 to Captain Robert Henry Sturgeon, an officer in the British army who was afterwards killed in the Peninsular War in 1813. Sarah unquestionably made it clear that her heart would always belong to the dead Emmet but that she would – and did – give her husband all her respect and affection.

Moore's lyric suggests that Sturgeon was not the only suitor:

> She is far from the land where her young
> hero sleeps,
> And lovers around her are sighing;
> But coldly she turns from their gaze and
> weeps
> For her heart in his grave is lying.

He seems to have been a kind and honourable man, and Sarah, without money or the capacity to earn it, felt that she could no longer be a burden on the Penroses. His regiment was ordered to Sicily and Sarah accompanied him to his billet in Messina. They left there ahead of the French army and moved back to England, to live briefly in Hythe, on the south-east coast of Kent. Sarah was tolerably happy in her marriage: in a letter to her friends Anne and Elizabeth Penrose written from Tangier on 24 October 1806, she writes: 'My dearest Henry . . . behaves like an angel to me.' A son ('a poor *little weak* child') was born on 26 December 1807 on the voyage home but died in Portsmouth on 10

January. Sarah remained ill, and died, probably of residual puerperal fever, on 3 May 1808. Her last letter (to Anne Penrose), written on 20 March, describes 'a hectic fever still upon me that so debilitates me that I am now barely able to walk across the room.' Sturgeon brought the body to Ireland, hoping that her father might relent and allow her to be buried, as she had requested, beside her sister Gertrude in the orchard of the Priory, but Curran refused. She rests in the churchyard of Newmarket, County Cork, her father's birthplace. It was the indefatigable Madden who found its location and erected a tombstone over it.

Moore was not her only memorialist; his friend the American essayist Washington Irving (1783–1859), whose best-known work *The Sketch Book of Geoffrey Crayon Gent* (1820) contains the stories 'Rip Van Winkle' and 'The Legend of Sleepy Hollow', devoted one of his pieces to the story of Robert and Sarah. In 'The Broken Heart' he expatiates on 'E——, the Irish patriot' whose 'fate made a deep impression on public sympathy . . . and even his enemies lamented the stern policy that dictated his execution.' He

finishes with the full text of Moore's melody.
From the point of view of subsequent history,
the most significant verse is the second:

> He had lived for his love, for his country
> he died –
> They were all that to life had entwined
> him –
> Nor soon shall the tears of his country be
> dried,
> Nor long shall his love stay behind him.

Emmet's reputation as the thoughtless, dashing
lover and romantic patriot was now firmly
established. He was to become, with Wolfe
Tone and the rest, the equivalent of a stained-
glass window in the chapel of later nationalism.
It was not the role he sought, nor does it fit the
facts. Whatever the reason for his taking command of the United Irishmen's second chance,
his brother Tom, Myles Byrne, Michael Dwyer
and Thomas Russell, veterans of earlier conflicts,
were happy to follow him. Russell could have
escaped to Scotland after the northern failure
but, with the persistence that illuminated his

whole life, came to Dublin hoping to organise Emmet's escape. He was betrayed by a spy to the police and arrested by Sirr on 9 September 1803. Sent to Downpatrick, County Down, on 12 October, he was tried by special commission on the twentieth. He was found guilty by a jury, of which six members, he noted, had once been United Irishmen, and hanged the next day. Russell lives on in ballad fame as 'the man they hanged in Downpatrick Gaol' in 'The Man from God-Knows-Where', written by Florence Mary Wilson (c. 1870–1946) in 1918.

Byrne escaped to France and served in the Irish Legion, just formed that year. He lost favour on the fall of Napoleon but was recalled to the French army in 1828. He resigned his commission in 1835, settled in Paris and left a vivid account of his life and times in post-humously published *Memoirs* (1863). Michael Dwyer, who had lived as an outlaw since 1789, surrendered voluntarily on 17 December 1803 and was sentenced to transportation to Botany Bay. He became high constable of Sydney in 1815 and died there in 1826. Jemmy Hope managed to remain in hiding in Dublin until

1806, when he returned to Belfast and took up again his old trade of linen-weaving. He survived until about 1846, having given Madden much information about the United Irish movement. Michael Quigley, the mobiliser of Kildare, who bore some responsibility for the hysteria that kept Emmet's men in the depot in the belief that the streets were full of troops, turned informer and was a useful ally to Trevor while in Kilmainham. Released in 1806, he bought a public house and drank the profits. McNally continued to live in Dublin, write plays and live comfortably on his secret government stipend of £300 a year in Harcourt Street until his death in 1820. The secret of his double life was revealed when an equally egregious son claimed a continuation of his father's dole.

Twenty-one men besides Emmet were executed and, with habeas corpus suspended, several thousand were thrown in prison and kept there until 1806, when the suspension lapsed. (One who died there of fever in 1805 was James Devlin, Anne's younger brother, who was allowed to live in Kilmainham because most of his family were prisoners there.) Emmet had been anxious not to involve any Catholics in the higher echelon of his movement; he appreciated their vulnerable position and did not want them to suffer any retaliatory punishment. Archbishop Troy (1739–1823) responded to the rising with an 'Exhortation', a sternly worded pastoral, to be read in all Dublin churches the morning after the disturbances. In it he urged Catholics to be aware of 'the many great benefits conferred on their body in this kingdom, during his present Majesty's auspicious reign' and condemned the 'outrageous contempt of [Hardwicke's] high authority and of the laws'. Yet the reaction from the Castle was the usual hysterical denunciation of the sacrament of Confession and the interrogation of Troy by Hardwicke on the nature of the seal of the sacrament, considering it 'to give every possible effect to detestable intrigue and treasonable conspiracies'.

This anti-Catholic attitude of the administration was maintained as it had been for more than a century, approved by the king in London, who could not find it consonant with his coronation oath to grant emancipation to those of the Romish persuasion. Orangeism continued to dominate Dublin politics, tacitly approved by the royal household. For more than a hundred years, the alternative to revolution – the agonisingly slow constitutionalism begun by O'Connell and carried on by Butt, Parnell and Redmond – had always to face the instinctive distrust by the British of the Catholic religion and the often violent opposition of the empowered Protestant minority at home. Low-key elements of revolution in the United Irishmen's tradition were visible in the rebellion of 1848, led by William Smith O'Brien, and later with the Fenian conspiracy. It was not, however, until the new century that any serious violence was again seen in Dublin, and by then Emmet, for long enshrined as the 'darling of Erin', was one of its patron saints.

It is hard to assess the events of the spring and summer of 1803. Its leader had undoubted charisma, as colleagues and adversaries alike confirmed. His attention to the mechanical details of his conspiracy was more successful than his sense of the feeling of the country. The swift reaction of the authorities gives some indication of how serious the threat to the establishment could have been if his general plans had been able to be implemented. The need to act prematurely and the almost obsessional regard for secrecy mean that few knew the overall strategy, and Emmet's ability as a commander was less than his capacity as a planner. Communications were poor and a sense of priorities that put the printed proclamations of the new republic above guns and explosives and held gorgeous uniforms for senior officers to be more important than a specific sequence of objectives was seriously flawed. The enterprise was dogged by misfortune, but then the thirty-six–year-old victor of Austerlitz, two years later, had his own views on luck. As Johnston described it in his introduction to the published play: 'It was very high-minded, and completely unsuccessful. It was picturesquely costumed, and insufficiently organised.'

The missing essential ingredient in the affair was French involvement; the country was disaffected, with at least 3 million adults who had nothing to lose by the ending of British rule. They might very well have joined an adequate invasion force and completed what Tone had attempted in 1796. As it was, nationalist Ireland lost a battle but gained another martyr; Irish popular theatre found a thrilling protagonist and the ballad-makers had a field day. Conceits such as the following, from a broadsheet, were common throughout the nineteenth century:

> But alas! he has gone, he is fallen a young
> flower.
> They have murdered my Emmet – my
> Emmet's no more.

And the chorus from Tom Maguire's ballad 'Bold Robert Emmet' may still be heard any Saturday night:

> Bold Robert Emmet, the darling of Erin,
> Bold Robert Emmet will die with a
> ssmile;
> Farewell companions both loyal and
> daring;
> I'll lay down my life for the Emerald Isle.

Perhaps the best summary of the persistence of the myth, as opposed to the history of the man, may be found in *The Clanking of the Chains* (1919),

Brinsley MacNamara's realistic novel of Irish country life in the early years of the last century:

> Yet were the people gripped, for no other reason than because it was a play about Robert Emmet. Indeed, Michael Dempsey need not have gone to such pains to give a great performance. Merely to have stood there on the very middle of the stage in his top boots with gold tassels, white trousers and black cut-away coat, his arms folded and a lock of hair brushed down upon his forehead, would have been quite sufficient. The drunken ballad-singers had told them all they wanted to know about Robert Emmet, and this was how they had always seen Robert Emmet dressed up in a picture.

SELECT BIBLIOGRAPHY

De Vere White, T. *Tom Moore*. London, 1977.

Elliott, M. *Partners in Revolution*. New Haven, 1982.

Landreth, H. *The Pursuit of Robert Emmet*. Dublin, 1949.

MacMullen, H. T. *The Voice of Sarah Curran*. Dublin, 1955.

Madden, R. R. *Memoir of Robert Emmet*. Dublin, 1846.

Moore, T. (ed. Lord John Russell). *Memoirs*. Vol. I. London, 1853.

Ó Broin, L. *The Unfortunate Mr Emmet*. Dublin, 1958.

Postgate, R. W. *Robert Emmet*. London, 1931.

Kee, R. *The Green Flag*. London, 1972